SandCastle™

Animal Homes

Home
Sweet
Nest

Mary Elizabeth Salzmann

CONSULTING EDITOR, DIANE CRAIG, M.A./READING SPECIALIST

A Division of ABDO

ABDO
Publishing Company

visit us at www.abdopublishing.com

Published by ABDO Publishing Company, a division of ABDO, P.O. Box 398166, Minneapolis, Minnesota 55439. Copyright © 2012 by Abdo Consulting Group, Inc. International copyrights reserved in all countries. No part of this book may be reproduced in any form without written permission from the publisher. SandCastle™ is a trademark and logo of ABDO Publishing Company.

Printed in the United States of America, North Mankato, Minnesota
062011
092011

 PRINTED ON RECYCLED PAPER

Editor: Katherine Hengel
Content Developer: Nancy Tuminelly
Cover and Interior Design and Production: Anders Hanson, Mighty Media, Inc.
Photo Credits: Shutterstock

Library of Congress Cataloging-in-Publication Data
Salzmann, Mary Elizabeth, 1968-
  Home sweet nest / Mary Elizabeth Salzmann.
    p. cm. -- (Animal homes)
  ISBN 978-1-61714-818-7
  1. Nest building--Juvenile literature. 2. Animals--Habitations--Juvenile literature. I. Title.
QL756.S26 2012
591.56´4--dc22
                    2010053272

SANDCASTLE™ LEVEL: TRANSITIONAL

SandCastle™ books are created by a team of professional educators, reading specialists, and content developers around five essential components—phonemic awareness, phonics, vocabulary, text comprehension, and fluency—to assist young readers as they develop reading skills and strategies and increase their general knowledge. All books are written, reviewed, and leveled for guided reading, early reading intervention, and Accelerated Reader® programs for use in shared, guided, and independent reading and writing activities to support a balanced approach to literacy instruction. The SandCastle™ series has four levels that correspond to early literacy development. The levels are provided to help teachers and parents select appropriate books for young readers.

Emerging Readers
(no flags)

Beginning Readers
(1 flag)

Transitional Readers
(2 flags)

Fluent Readers
(3 flags)

Contents

What Is a Nest?

Birds and other animals build nests. Animals make nests with sticks, leaves, fur, and other things they find.

Nests are often in high places such as trees or cliffs. But they can be on the ground too.

Animals and Nests

Nests **protect** eggs and babies. Some animals lay their eggs and then never return to the nest. Other animals stay with their young until they are grown up.

Bald eagles live in nests.

Bald eagles build the largest nests of any bird in North America. Their nests are in the tops of tall trees near rivers, lakes, or oceans.

Flamingos build nests.

Flamingos make their nests out of mud. The flamingo builds a pile of mud with its beak. Then it smooths it with its feet. It makes a hole in the top for the eggs.

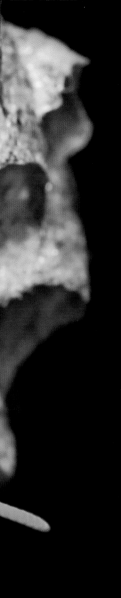

Paper wasps build nests.

Paper wasps chew on
bits of wood and plants.
This makes a thin, papery
material. Then they use the
material to build their nests.

Storks live in nests.

Storks build large nests in trees or on buildings. Storks **migrate**, but they return to the same nest.

Termites build nests.

Termites build large nests. They can be underground or in logs or trees. Some termite nests grow into huge mounds.

Masked weavers live in nests.

Male masked weavers use grass and other plants to **weave** nests. Then the **females** line the nests with grass and feathers.

Alligators build nests.

Alligators use plants to make nests on the ground. The **female** alligator lays eggs in the nest. She **protects** the nest until the babies **hatch**. The babies leave the nest after they hatch.

Could *you*
live in a nest?

Quiz

1. A nest can be on the ground.
True or false?

2. Nests **protect** eggs and babies.
True or false?

3. Flamingos make their nests out of mud. *True or false?*

4. Termite nests are small.
True or false?

5. Baby alligators stay in the nest after they **hatch**. *True or false?*

Glossary

female – being of the sex that can produce eggs or give birth. Mothers are female.

hatch – to break out of an egg.

male – being of the sex that can father offspring. Fathers are male.

material – something that other things can be made of.

migrate – to move from one place to another, usually at about the same time each year.

protect – to guard someone or something from harm or danger.

weave – to make something by passing strips of material over and under each other.